The World of Composers

Mozart

Greta Cencetti

PETER BEDRICK BOOKS

McGraw-Hill
Children's Publishing
A Division of The McGraw-Hill Companies

This edition published in the United States in 2002 by
Peter Bedrick Books, an imprint of
McGraw-Hill Children's Publishing,
A Division of The McGraw-Hill Companies
8787 Orion Place
Columbus, Ohio 43240

www.MHkids.com

ISBN 1-58845-471-1

Library of Congress Cataloging-in-Publication Data

Cencetti, Greta.
Mozart / Greta Cencetti.
p. cm. -- (The world of composers)
Summary: An introduction to the life and musical career
of the eighteenth-century Austrian composer.
ISBN 1-58845-471-1
1. Mozart, Wolfgang Amadeus, 1756-1791--Juvenile literature. 2. Composers—
Austria—Biography—Juvenile literature. [1. Mozart, Wolfgang Amadeus,
1756-1791. 2. Composers.] I. Title. II. Series.

ML3930.M9 C46 2002
780'.92--dc21
[B]
2001052558

© 2002 Ta Chien Publishing Co., Ltd.
© 2002 Studio Mouse

10 9 8 7 6 5 4 3 2 1 CHRT 06 05 04 03 02

Printed in China.

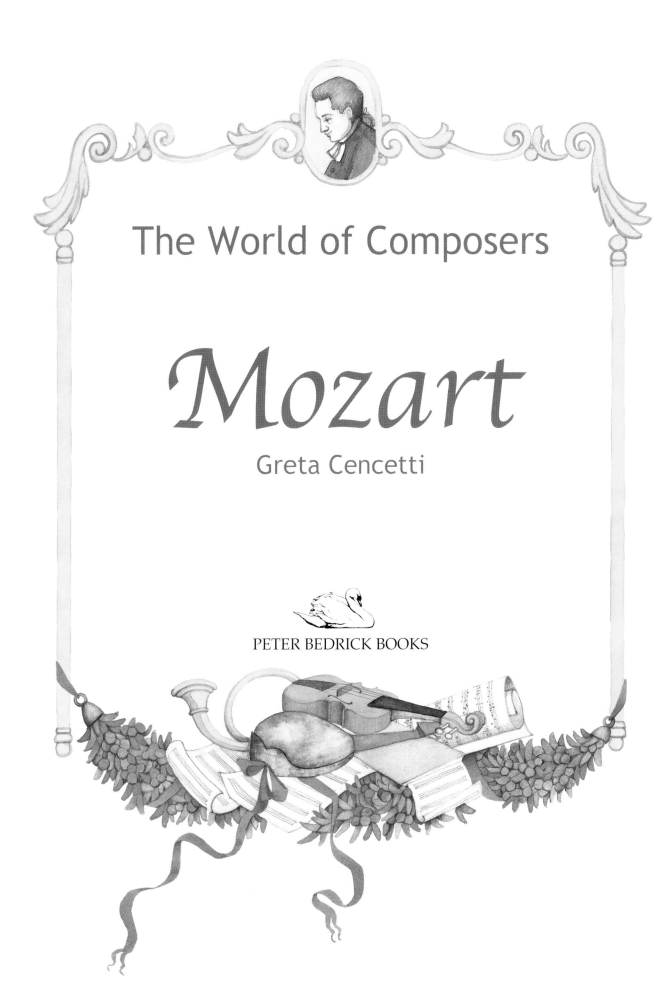

The World of Composers

Mozart

Greta Cencetti

PETER BEDRICK BOOKS

Contents

Europe

SALZ

Chapter 1
The Mozart Family

Wolfgang Amadeus Mozart (pronounced MOHT-sahrt) was born on January 27, 1756, in Salzburg, Austria. He was the son of Leopold and Anna Maria Mozart.

Mozart's father was concertmaster for the court orchestra of the archbishop of Salzburg. Leopold Mozart was considered to be an outstanding musician. He wrote several compositions for the violin.

From birth, Wolfgang was surrounded by music. His sister, Maria Anna, known as Nannerl, began to play the piano at an early age, and so did young Wolfgang. In fact, he learned to play the piano at almost the same time he learned to walk.

By the age of four, Mozart was already a good pianist. By the time he was five, he started to play a miniature violin, which had been made especially for him. Young Mozart enjoyed playing the piano and the violin more than any other activity. It wasn't long before he was composing his own music.

Chapter 2
A Child Prodigy

Mozart's father realized then that his son was a musical genius. He decided to take the little boy, along with the rest of the family, on a concert tour of Europe. They traveled to Monaco, Vienna, Paris, and London, as well as Italy, Germany, and Holland.

Mozart and his sister, Nannerl, performed for the royal families of each of the cities and countries they visited. Many of the people who heard the young genius could not believe how a boy of his age could play so well.

Audiences would often ask Mozart to shut his eyes and play. He never missed a note, proving how musically gifted he was. Young Mozart also impressed people with his ability to play an entire piece of music after hearing it only once.

Mozart soon gained the admiration of Europe's royal class. The Queen of Austria was especially impressed with the young musician.

Chapter 3
A Star in Europe

When Mozart was 14, he went to St. Peter's Church in Rome with his father. There, he gave a concert performance. One of the most popular hymns of the time was "Lord, I Need Thy Tenderness." The bishop owned the copyright for this song, and no one was allowed to copy it. Mozart listened to the song once and memorized the notes. Then, he wrote it down on a piece of paper and mischievously hid it under his wig.

By the time Mozart was 18, he had traveled extensively throughout Europe. He made many friends, including artists and politicians, and he won the admiration and respect of nobility and royalty.

He continued his musical studies in Italy, and he was often asked to compose operas and other works of music. Although his performances were a great success, musicians usually were not paid very well.

Chapter 4
Mozart Meets Aloysia

In 1777, Mozart traveled with his mother to Paris for a performance. On the way, they passed through the German city of Mannheim. There, Mozart met the Weber family.

Aloysia, the oldest daughter, had a beautiful voice, and Mozart soon fell in love with her. He abandoned his travels and neglected his performances. This hurt his chances of becoming the well-paid, famous musician that he could be.

Mozart wrote a letter to his father, telling him that he wanted to marry Aloysia. Leopold opposed the marriage. He insisted that Mozart leave for Paris immediately with his mother.

Aloysia was not interested in marrying Mozart. She was more intent on becoming a famous singer. Mozart and his mother eventually left Mannheim and the Weber household for Paris.

Chapter 5
A Time of Misfortune

Life in Paris was not as promising as Mozart hoped it would be. Though he continued performing and composing, he was not as popular as he once had been. He could barely make ends meet. Things grew worse after his mother fell ill and then died.

Mozart decided to return to Salzburg. He took a position as the organist in the court orchestra of the Archbishop of Salzburg.

HIERONYMUS   COLLOREDO ✝

1772

The archbishop, named Colloredo, was an extremely powerful ruler of Salzburg. He was displeased that Mozart was often away on concert tours.

The archbishop insisted that Mozart stay in Salzburg and work exclusively for him, but Mozart didn't want to work for someone who dictated his every move. Fortunately, Mozart's newest opera, *Idomeneo*, was performed in Vienna and was very successful. After a dispute with the archbishop, Mozart left Salzburg and traveled to Vienna.

Chapter 6
Constanze, Mozart's Great Love

Although Mozart was popular in Vienna, he still was not making much money. It was difficult for him to find a place to live that he could afford. The Weber sisters were also living in Vienna, so he joined them in their home. Aloysia was now married and had established a career as a singer.

Mozart worked hard composing new pieces and teaching music to earn more money. He also won a piano competition. At last, he was earning the money he needed to live on.

Shortly thereafter, Mozart fell in love with the youngest daughter in the Weber family, Constanze. They were married on August 4, 1782. This was a happy period of time for Mozart, and he composed several operas for the opera house in Vienna.

Chapter 7
The Genius Behind the Operas

At the age of 30, Mozart created one of his most famous operas, *The Marriage of Figaro*. He had become friends with a writer, Lorenzo da Ponte, who wrote the text for *The Marriage of Figaro*. They worked together to create another well-known opera, *Don Giovanni*. This famous opera takes place in Spain and tells the complicated story of Don Giovanni and his trickery.

As Mozart developed new musical ideas, the people in Vienna became less enthusiastic about his work. Some say it was because the nobility disliked the radical ideas in *Figaro*. Others say it was because the people's tastes in music had changed.

Whatever the case, Mozart found a better audience in the Czechoslovakian city of Prague. There, the opera *Don Giovanni* was first performed in 1787.

As Mozart's musical career developed, he had increasingly less respect for royal families and stopped seeking their financial support. Mozart and his family lived in poverty. He and Constanze had six children, but four of them died in infancy. Mozart struggled to earn a living, and he sometimes had to borrow money just to survive.

Mozart was also plagued by poor health, but he continued to compose to earn money. He worked at home during the day and sometimes met his friends from the opera house during the evening.

Chapter 8
The Magic Flute

Among Mozart's friends was Emanuel Schikaneder, a gentleman who managed a theater in Vienna. Schikaneder paid Mozart to write an opera called *The Magic Flute*. This legendary opera tells the story of a princess in distress who needed to be rescued from the evil Queen of the Night. In the most exciting part of the story, the prince, who is trying to rescue the princess, plays a flute. The magical song of the flute leads to the rescue of the princess. At the end of the opera, the prince and the princess marry.

At that time, operas were usually performed in opera houses, and only the nobility attended. *The Magic Flute* is said to be the first opera composed for the common people because it was performed in a theater rather than in an opera house. Though it was unusual to stage an opera in a theater, Mozart knew it was an opportunity for him to earn money for his family.

Chapter 9
A Mysterious Visitor

*A*s Mozart's health worsened, he stayed in bed for longer periods, but this did not stop him from composing new songs.

Near the end of his life, a strange thing happened. One day, a man who wore black clothes and covered his face, appeared at Mozart's house.

This mysterious man gave Mozart a bag of gold and asked that he compose a requiem, or funeral piece. Although the offer seemed strange, Mozart needed the money to support his family. Because he was ill, he managed to finish only three-quarters of the piece. He explained the general theme of the work to one of his students, who completed it.

Chapter 10
The Burial of a Pauper

By chance, the last piece of music that Mozart composed was the requiem. Wolfgang Amadeus Mozart died on December 5, 1792, at the young age of 35. He was buried in an unmarked grave, as was the tradition in Vienna at the time.

Though Mozart died a poor man, he left behind the riches of his operas, symphonies, and church music for the world to treasure.

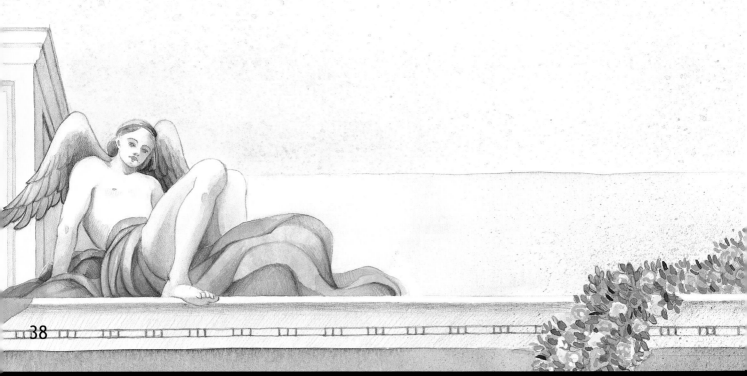

Introduction to the Strings

*T*he violin, one of the main instruments in the string family, played an important role in Mozart's musical beginnings. In addition to the violin, the viola, the cello, and the double bass are the other principal instruments in the string family.

The string family forms the basis of the symphony orchestra. A typical symphony orchestra consists of 30 violins, 12 violas, 12 cellos, and 8 double basses. Other various wind and percussion instruments are added to this, depending on what is needed for a specific piece of music.

All string instruments have four strings and are made of wood. A thin strip of wood, called the *fingerboard*, covers the neck and part of the body. The strings are connected to the violin at the *scroll*, or top of the violin, and the *tail*, or the bottom. They are held tightly in place by a cork *bridge* and wooden *pegs*.

The violin is the smallest and highest pitched string instrument, followed by the viola. The versions of the violin and viola we see today originated in the mid-1500s and are held between the chin and shoulder.

String instruments are played by drawing a *bow* (usually made of wood and horsehair) over the strings. The bow is pressed against the strings but without too much pressure, which would produce a scratchy tone. The strings can also be plucked over the fingerboard with the index finger of the right hand.

The cello is constructed almost the same way, but it is held between the knees, rather than on the shoulder. Both the cello and the double bass stand on the floor and are supported by a thin metal piece, called a *endpin*. These instruments have low, deep sounds.

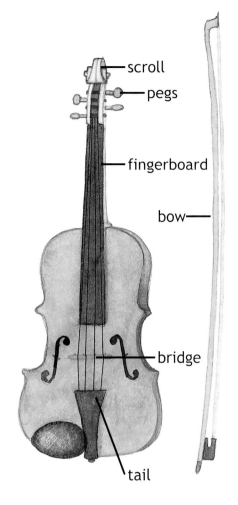

scroll
pegs
fingerboard
bow
bridge
tail

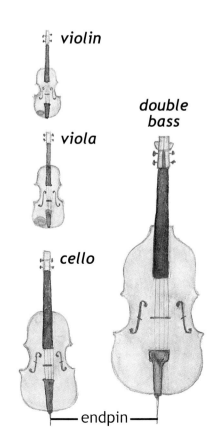

violin
viola
cello
double bass
endpin